AMY POEHLER

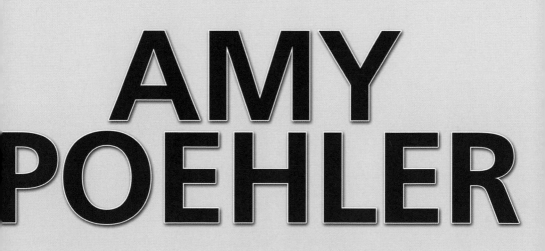

JUSTINE CIOVACCO

THE
GIANTS
OF COMEDY™

AMY
POEHLER

JUSTINE CIOVACCO

ROSEN
PUBLISHING®

New York

Published in 2016 by The Rosen Publishing Group, Inc.
29 East 21st Street, New York, NY 10010

First Edition

Library of Congress Cataloging-in-Publication Data

Ciovacco, Justine.
 Amy Poehler / Justine Ciovacco. -- First edition
     pages cm. -- (The giants of comedy)
 Includes bibliographical references and index.
 ISBN 978-1-4994-6258-6 (library bound)
 1. Poehler, Amy, 1971---Juvenile literature. 2. Actors--United States--
Biography--Juvenile literature. I. Title.
 PN2287.P565C56 2016
 792.702'8092--dc23
 [B]
                                                2015025508

Manufactured in China

CONTENTS

6 INTRODUCTION

9 CHAPTER **ONE** From Birth to Burlington to Broadway (Sort Of)

18 CHAPTER **TWO** Finding Improv and Inspiration at College

26 CHAPTER **THREE** Learning the Ropes in Chicago

38 CHAPTER **FOUR** Expanding Her Audience—and Mind—in New York

50 CHAPTER **FIVE** Ladies and Gentlemen, It's Saturday Night!

60 CHAPTER **SIX** Getting Personal

71 CHAPTER **SEVEN** This Mother's Work Is Never Done

84 **Fact Sheet on Amy Poehler**
85 **Fact Sheet on Amy Poehler's Work**
90 **Critical Reviews**
92 **Timeline**
95 **Glossary**
98 **For More Information**
101 **For Further Reading**
103 **Bibliography**
109 **Index**

INTRODUCTION

Amy Poehler, pictured with her character from Disney-Pixar's *Inside Out* at the 2015 movie premiere, has been making audiences laugh—and think—for decades.

By simply following her dreams, Amy Poehler has provided a lot of laughs and inspiration. She was always a huge fan of female comedy stars, such as *Saturday Night Live* cast member Gilda Radner and sketch comedy TV icon Carol Burnett. So it was no wonder she was fascinated by the world of improvisational comedy after she got a taste of that kind of work in her time at Boston College. The hard work needed to make performing look easy and the ability to be open to the ideas of others were just as appealing to Poehler. With friends by her side, Poehler moved to Chicago after college. There, she immersed herself in the thriving improv community and learned from many of the best minds in the business at improv outlets such as Second City and ImprovOlympic. She joined with friends to form the Upright Citizens Brigade and traveled the country performing. They then took their chances moving to New York City to see if they could find new ways to showcase their talents and add to the city's growing improvisational comedy scene.

As a performer and writer (and often as a waitress), Poehler always found work, and she has always found the improv community to be an excellent power source for her ideas. Her writing and performance work on *Saturday Night Live* (*SNL*) made her a household name, and the work she has done since then—in TV, in film, online, and in published media—has broadened her audience.

Poehler's background in improv has also encouraged her love of working with others and giving new artists a push. She sees more directing and producing in her future so she can open doors to give attention to other uniquely creative minds.

More personally, Poehler's work has also given her the platform to encourage self-esteem in young people. The Smart Girls organization she cofounded helps young women find positive influences online, and it marries the ideas that have made Poehler so popular—enjoying each other's sense of humor, building a sense of community, and appreciating hard work.

Amy Poehler's popularity is based not just on her hilarious portrayals of an overly cheerful deputy parks director, singer Michael Jackson, politician Hillary Clinton, former North Korean leader Kim Jong-Il, and a one-legged, hyperactive, farting girl named Amber, among many others. It means something to the audience that she can not only deliver a great line but also write one. Amy Poehler has very many fans because she takes risks, and her audience feels good watching her do it.

CHAPTER **ONE**

From Birth to Burlington to Broadway (Sort Of)

On September 16, 1971, Eileen Poehler gave birth to Amy Meredith in Newton, Massachusetts. The twenty-four-year-old had been married to Amy's father, twenty-four-year-old Bill, for only eleven months. They met at a state college, where he was captain of the basketball team and she was captain of the cheerleaders. Socially, this was a different time for women. It was something that Amy's mother, Eileen, pointed out to Amy many times over the years. The fact that this mattered to both Amy and her mother would shape Amy's outlook years later, as she not only found her way in the somewhat male-dominated field of comedy but also found that her knowledge and power could be a benefit to young women.

GUNKA AND NANA

Amy grew up living near her mother's parents, Steve and Helen Milmore. To Amy, they were Gunka and Nana.

Steve was a firefighter who served as a machine gunner in World War II. After he married Helen, he served overseas for five years before returning home and never speaking about the war. The couple had three children, and they adored their grandchildren and were beloved in return.

Steve died in 1982 when Amy was ten, and Helen died in 2003. The Wurlitzer organ that Steve loved to play with his grandchildren on his lap now sits in Amy's New York City apartment. Her sons play it. "They sit on the same bench I sat on and feel the same good feelings of family and home," Amy wrote in her book *Yes, Please.*

On the day of Amy's birth, Bill took Eileen to the hospital after her contractions started and left to await the birth at Eileen's parents' house. As was fairly common at the time, Eileen was given anesthesia, fell asleep, and woke up with a baby.

Early Life

Eileen, who had been working as a third grade teacher when she became pregnant, knew her school's policy was that she should resign upon finding out she was pregnant. Her principal allowed

Poehler poses with actress Tatiana Maslany and her first book, *Yes, Please*, at a 2014 book signing in Toronto, Canada.

her to work through the school year, but she resigned the summer before Amy was born so she could be a stay-at-home mom. The women's movement was taking shape and the National Organization for Women had just formed, but society as a whole still believed that women should stay home with their children, and Eileen felt that push to be a full-time mom. In a passage she wrote in Amy's 2014 book, *Yes, Please*, Eileen noted that she felt she had to because her parents were still working, there was no day care available nearby, and it was the "right thing" to do. "For me, it just wasn't socially acceptable to go back to work full-time," she said, "and I had always followed the rules."

Bill Poehler, also a teacher at the time, was thrilled with the birth of his first child. "I have never forgotten holding you as a newborn," he wrote teasingly in *Yes, Please*, "with your whole fanny fitting in the palm of my hand."

Baby Amy had three years of her parents' full attention before her brother, Greg, was born. When Amy was five, her family moved to Burlington, Massachusetts. There, 12 miles (19 kilometers) northwest of Boston, Eileen became much more active outside the home, busy with other full-time moms who volunteered to make Burlington better. They made paths for a walking trail, delivered meals to the sick and elderly, and built floats for the annual Fourth of July parade. Amy and her brother were often by Eileen's side as she carved out a fulfilling social life. Bill was active in the town, too. Not only did Amy and her brother learn the importance of taking part in a community, but they also saw their mom become her own person, motivated and adaptable to the world around her.

Ready for Attention

Amy was always feisty, confident, and a natural "activity nerd" who loved being with friends. Her parents, she told the *Wall Street Journal* in 2011, "gave me the feeling as a kid that there wasn't anything I couldn't do."

Her father remembers that he saw Amy's confidence early on. When she was in second grade and was dressed as a snowflake for a winter pageant, she approached the microphone on stage to recite a poem after the principal had just spoken and left the microphone up high. "Little Amy walks across [the stage], goes up to the mike, grabs the little knob, twists it, pulls it down, and I said to myself, 'Oh God, she has no stage fright whatsoever.'"

That confidence helped ten-year-old Amy win the role of Dorothy in Wildwood Elementary School's production of *The Wizard of Oz*. That role, Amy points out, is where she first learned the joys of improvisational acting—and of getting a big laugh.

Before playing Dorothy, the fourth-grader had been onstage only twice before, once in the winter pageant and another time in third grade as a singing lion. This time was different because she needed to do something that wasn't planned. Caught up in a tornado, she was supposed to call out for her lost dog (a real poodle!), Toto, but she was holding the dog as she called out, "Toto, Toto! Where are you?" The audience laughed. Rather than feeling embarrassed, Amy loved it and decided that she'd actually try to make people laugh at the second night's performance. That night, she held the dog until her line and then put it down and walked a few feet away before saying the line. The dog sat still, and Amy got big laughs.

At Burlington High School, Amy enjoyed floating in and out of different activities. Her school was large, with four hundred people in her graduating class. She was involved in basketball, softball, soccer, and student council.

Amy also got a first job at age sixteen. She and many of her friends knew they were expected to find work to save up for college and the extra costs that come with having a social life. She first found work as a junior secretary in a podiatrist's office near home. The summer before she started college, she found another job, serving as a waitress at Chadwick's, a restaurant and ice cream parlor in nearby Lexington.

CAROL BURNETT: A PIONEERING TV COMEDY STAR

Carol Creighton Burnett, born April 26, 1933, in San Antonio, Texas, is best known for her TV variety show, *The Carol Burnett Show*. She was raised by her grandmother, Mabel, because her alcoholic parents couldn't take care of her and her younger half-sister, Chrissie. They lived in a boarding house in a run-down area of Hollywood, California, not far from her mother.

She studied theater arts and English at the

Comedy legend Carol Burnett's improvisational comedy style influenced Amy Poehler.

(continued on the next page)

(continued from the previous page)

University of California, Los Angeles, and then moved to New York to find work as an actress. After a number of comedy roles on TV, she originated the role of Princess Winnifred in the comedic play *Once Upon a Mattress* on Broadway and was nominated for a Tony.

Carol Burnett won her first Emmy the following year playing a multitude of different characters on the comedy-variety show *The Garry Moore Show*. Her own variety show was the first to be led by a woman. It ran on CBS from 1967 to 1978 and was awarded twenty-three Emmys. The show still airs on TV in syndication under the name *Carol Burnett and Friends*. She has also had a number of popular Broadway and film roles, including Miss Hannigan in the 1982 film of the musical *Annie*.

There, she was happy to sing and dance, as was always done on a customer's birthday.

In her senior year of high school, Amy won the role of Princess Winnifred in the school's version of *Once Upon a Mattress*. This was a big deal for Amy because one of her comedy heroes, Carol Burnett, originated the role on Broadway. Amy remembers the role as having a lot of loud singing. She also enjoyed the frantic energy that went with the performance—rushing costume changes, playing to a live

Jane Connell plays Princess Winnifred, the role originally played by Carol Burnett, in a 1960 performance of *Once Upon a Mattress* at London's Adelphi Theatre. Poehler was cast in a high school production of the show.

audience, feeling stressed, and making last-minute changes. For the first time, she thought about some-day being an actress.

CHAPTER TWO

Finding Improv and Inspiration at College

After graduating from high school, Poehler became a communications major at Boston College. Unlike her parents, she wasn't planning on becoming a teacher, and that was okay with them. "Although it's an awful thing to say, and I think she would have been a fabulous teacher, I might have been silently a little disappointed if she went into teaching," her mother, Eileen, told the *Wall Street Journal* in 2011. Instead, her parents figured their outgoing daughter would probably become a newscaster or a reporter.

A Different World

College was a new and bigger world for Poehler, and she was ready for it. Still, she was surprised

Poehler returned to Boston College in 2006 for an interview with students. She is pictured with the then-director of My Mother's Fleabag, Katy Hagen.

at the school's diverse population of about fourteen thousand students from different parts of the country and around the world. She felt a bit awkward that many of the students seemed to come from backgrounds that were wealthier than that of her solid middle-class family.

It was 1989 when Poehler started college, so she styled her hair big, like her friends back home.

Her hair was loaded with hairspray, and she often completed her look with big shoulder pads, chunky earrings, thick belts, and tight stretch pants—all the style of the time for many people, but especially big among Poehler and her high school friends. However, that style coupled with her Boston accent made Poehler feel like she stood out in ways she didn't want to in this new setting with all new people around her. The typical Boston accent includes the use of "lazy Rs." As Poehler describes it in *Yes, Please*, "Our mouths never close and we sound like big, lazy babies." She made the decision to tone down her style and work on the accent.

In her first week of freshman orientation, Poehler went to a performance at the Eagles Nest, a campus cafeteria and social center. A student group called My Mother's Fleabag was giving an improvisational comedy performance in which they all got into the act, making quick jokes and bouncing ideas off each other. Poehler loved the show and met one of the performers, Kara McNamara, who encouraged her to audition to be in the group.

Starting in Theater

Poehler was accepted by and performed with My Mother's Fleabag in the few shows they put on each year. Despite a low performance schedule, they rehearsed constantly and would spend

WHAT IS IMPROVISATIONAL THEATER?

Improvisational theater, often called improv, features performers who create most of what they will say and do on the spot while performing in front of an audience. Good improv, however, is often the result of good actors who have a natural comfort with each other, usually due to a lot of rehearsal and experience performing while feeding off each other's ideas. Good improvisers are quick thinkers and good listeners, who can react to things as they happen.

The art of improv goes back at least to ancient Rome with pieces in verse, sometimes accompanied by dance. Modern improvisational performances are largely based on the work of vaudeville performers in the United States and Canada, who would travel from theater to theater in the 1880s to 1930s with an act that became part of a larger performance in which different performers would entertain in any way possible—acting, singing, juggling, dancing, and so on. Many performers tried to get audience members involved in order to hold the audience's attention. They could do this by allowing the audience to name themes, settings, and personality types they would then incorporate into their act.

One of the earliest groups to gain popularity as improv performers was the Compass Players, a cabaret theater that was active in Chicago, Illinois, and St. Louis, Missouri, between 1955 and 1958. Several members of the group went on to form the now legendary Second City theater, a launch pad for many modern comedy performers, in Chicago in 1959.

hours arguing over one joke. They mainly acted in sketches, took the lead on games, and sang songs, often about Boston College topics, because that's what their audience could relate to. Poehler loved the relationships she formed in the group and was hooked on the audience's reactions.

She and McNamara moved off campus with a bunch of friends. The group of friends would regularly host big parties, sometimes with dress-up themes like Goodbye to the Eighties. Meeting more and more of the diverse student population helped Poehler learn about the world, especially artists and writers she had never heard of. She attended classes during the day and spent many nights writing sketches. "I huddled with a bunch of misfits and practiced being stupid on purpose," she explained in *Yes, Please*.

Of course, she also had to earn money to pay for the more exciting social life she was experiencing. She found work once again as a waitress, this time at Papa Razzi, an Italian restaurant and bar.

At this point Poehler wasn't sure what kind of acting she might do, but she knew what she didn't want to do. She didn't want to feel tied down or stuck in somewhat traditional social roles—yet. She knew money, marriage, stability, and children would not be part of at least the next ten years of her life.

Planning for the Future

One night in Poehler's junior year, McNamara told her she planned to move to Chicago after graduation. She was a year ahead of Poehler and eager to try to get more improvisational acting experience. McNamara's goal was to take classes with the well-known comedy troupe Second City, which had theaters in Chicago and Toronto.

GILDA RADNER: *SNL* TO BROADWAY

When Poehler graduated from high school, her aunt gave her a card that said, "I'll see you on *Saturday Night Live!*" She may have been joking, but she knew one of Poehler's comedy heroes, Gilda Radner, hit it big on *SNL.*

Gilda Susan Radner was born on June 28, 1946, in Detroit, Michigan. She attended the University of Michigan at Ann Arbor but dropped out in her senior year to move to Toronto with her boyfriend. There, she made her stage debut in the musical *Godspell*, featuring future stars such as Martin Short, who later became an *SNL* cast member. She and Short also joined Toronto's Second City comedy troupe. Radner followed that up with a featured role on the *National Lampoon Radio*

(continued on the next page)

23

(continued from the previous page)

Gilda Radner's enthusiastic energy and comedic timing made *Gilda Radner: Live from New York* a hit on Broadway in 1979. She is pictured on opening night.

Hour, where she became friends with future *SNL* stars Bill Murray, John Belushi, and Chevy Chase.

In 1975, Radner became one of *SNL*'s first cast members. She stayed with the show for five years, creating memorable characters such as an annoying advice expert named Roseanne Rosannadanna and Baba Wawa, a parody of TV journalist Barbara Walters. She won an Emmy for her *SNL* work in 1977; had a successful one-woman Broadway show, *Gilda Radner: Live from New York*; and starred in film comedies, including three with her second husband, actor Gene Wilder.

Radner died of ovarian cancer on May 20, 1989. The national cancer wellness community Gilda's Club was started by Wilder and her friends in her memory.

After some research, Poehler and her friend found that ImprovOlympic—a theater group that features long-form improvisational acts, rather than short sketches—also had classes. The plan was set for McNamara to move to Chicago and get an apartment, and then Poehler would join her after she graduated from college.

Whatever Makes You Happy

Poehler's parents, who had remortgaged their small Burlington home twice to pay for their children's college education, felt a bit unclear on what career path she might take. When she graduated and was still sure she wanted more training as an improvisational comedian, they worried, mostly silently. "Oh, that's great. Do whatever makes you happy, honey," Bill Poehler remembers saying, according to an interview in the *Wall Street Journal.* This was after his daughter confirmed what she planned to do after college. Her parents kept their worry between themselves. "We walk into the other room, look at each other, and say, 'Oh my God! We just spent all that money and now she's going to be an actress?'"

Poehler's parents were concerned that it would be hard to make money and find a career as an improvisational actress. And it was hard, but Poehler was on the right path.

CHAPTER THREE

Learning the Ropes in Chicago

After graduating college in 1993, Poehler moved to Chicago to sharpen her improv skills. She quickly found work as a waitress. Again.

At the fine-dining restaurant Carlucci, Poehler and the other servers wore burgundy vests and floral ties. She saw incredibly popular TV host Oprah Winfrey eat there and opened wines worth hundreds of dollars for customers with big money to spend.

She found a beautiful but cheap apartment in a "scary" neighborhood with her friend Kara McNamara from Boston College and another friend, Martin Gobbee. Her dad helped her move by driving McNamara's Jeep from Massachusetts to Chicago, loaded with their belongings.

Poehler often rode her bike to see improv shows. Chicago was then—and still is—a major training ground for comedy talent. The first time Poehler saw a Second City show, she saw three people who would later become huge comedy stars: Amy Sedaris, Stephen Colbert, and Steve Carell. Colbert's big break came via the Comedy Central late-night news satire *The Daily Show*; he then created a conservative character when he was given his own TV show, *The Colbert Report*, which ran until late 2014. Following that, he dropped the conservative persona that had made him famous to host *The Late Show* on CBS. Carell, Oscar-nominated

AMY SEDARIS: SKETCH COMEDY GODDESS

Amy Poehler has said this about Amy Sedaris: "When it comes to sketch, I don't think I've ever seen anyone funnier." Amy Louise Sedaris was born in Endicott, New York, on March 29, 1961. She and her five siblings, including popular satire writer David Sedaris, grew up in Raleigh, North Carolina.

After sharpening her improv skills with Second City and other troupes, Sedaris moved to New York

(continued on the next page)

(continued from the previous page)

Actress Amy Sedaris is known for her quick wit and hilarious characters.

to work on the Comedy Central sketch show *Exit 57*, which ran from 1995 to 1998 and also starred Stephen Colbert. She then joined *Strangers with Candy*, a Comedy Central show in which she played a forty-six-year-old runaway high school dropout who returns to school. She starred in a 2006 film of the same name.

Sedaris has written a comedic craft book (2010's *Simple Times: Crafts for Poor People!*) and numerous plays with her brother David. She has had small roles in dozens of films and TV shows and has also made memorable late-night talk show appearances, cracking up David Letterman, Jimmy Kimmel, and Conan O'Brien, among others. For a time, she also ran a cheese ball and cupcake business called Dusty Food Cupcakes out of her home kitchen in New York City.

for the 2015 drama *Foxcatcher*, has had a number of successful film comedy roles and a lead role in the TV comedy *The Office*, for which he received six lead actor Emmy nominations.

A Different Kind of Education

Poehler began taking improv classes—acting out scenes and studying different forms of improv through games, songs, word association, and more. Still, like every performer, she wanted to be onstage. She got her chance when she joined the theater group ImprovOlympic (now called iO). In its small theater with about one hundred seats, the group had a regular half-hour performance that was like a "midnight improv jam."

The midnight shows were eye-opening for Poehler, who learned a lot about herself while performing in front of a noncollege audience. "Sometimes I turned into a desperate joke machine. Other times, I got shy and passive," she explains in *Yes, Please*, noting sometimes she would find herself acting "weirdly physical or sexual." "When people are nervous and put on the spot, they tend to show you who they really are."

Poehler was learning the rules of long-form improvisation—not just short sketches. In long-form improv, a one-word suggestion from the audience can turn into a whole show. Poehler was still a student, but now a paying audience was watching. "I loved that improv was about collaboration and coming from a place of yes," she explained to *Elle* magazine in 2014.

The "yes" aspect of improv is important. It means staying open-minded and agreeable to other performers and their ideas—and to the audience's participation. A good improviser must be a good listener and support his or her partners in the performance. You are essentially finding a game you and your partner can play together.

ImprovOlympic had a free-form style onstage, but—like all troupes—they took training seriously. It

DEL CLOSE: THE GODFATHER OF IMPROV

Del Close pioneered long-form improvisation, in which performers create an entire show consisting of interconnected scenes, characters, and ideas completely made up on the spot with no preplanning or prewriting. Born on March 9, 1934, and raised in Manhattan, Kansas, Del Close developed his sense of humor while dealing with the issues that come with having an alcoholic father.

He attended Kansas State University and enjoyed acting. At twenty-three, he became a member of the improvisational comedy revue the Compass Players in St. Louis, Missouri. He followed when most of the cast—including a comedy team that later gained huge popularity, Elaine May and Mike Nichols (who also became an Oscar-winning director)—moved to New York City. After learning and performing there, he moved to Chicago in 1960.

In Chicago, he performed and directed at the Second City theater until he was fired because of substance abuse. He returned to Chicago's Second City in 1972 and became a mentor to many comedic actors. Among the many stars he guided are Amy Sedaris, Stephen Colbert (*The Colbert Report/Late Show with Stephen Colbert*), Eric Stonestreet (*Modern Family*), and *SNL* stars Bill Murray, Gilda Radner, John Belushi, Tina Fey, Mike Meyers, Tim Meadows, John Candy, and Chris Farley. He died on March 4, 1999, of emphysema.

was run by Charna Halpern, who Poehler calls her first real improv teacher, and Halpern's husband, Del Close. Halpern put teams together, decided who moved to different team levels, and had the exhausting task of running the theater. Close was a behind-the-scenes comedy genius, having coached numerous future comedy stars, especially those who went on to become featured players on *Saturday Night Live*.

Meeting Future Colleagues

As part of her improv training, Poehler would watch ImprovOlympic's most seasoned members, called the Family, perform in nightly shows. She'd marvel at their talent and then write notes, such as "Amy, take more risks!" and "Don't be afraid to sing!" in her journal.

It was in Chicago that former *SNL* regular and current *Late Night* talk show host Seth Meyers first saw Poehler perform. At the time, in the mid-1990s, she was at ImprovOlympic, where the group often tried to get its small audience involved. She and the others were playing a game called "The Dream." Poehler selected Meyers after he raised his hand when she asked if there was an audience member who would come onstage and tell about his or her day. "My first conversation with Amy was in front of an audience: me in a chair, her standing beside me. She was charming, funny, sweet, and sharp, and I left thinking, 'I would like to be her friend,'" he remembers in a chapter he wrote for her book, *Yes, Please*.

It was also in Chicago that Poehler met a fellow lover of improv from Upper Darby, Pennsylvania. Tina Fey, who was a year older than Poehler, graduated from the University of Virginia with a drama degree and experience as a playwright. She moved to Chicago to become part of the Chicago arm of the comedy troupe the Second City and also worked with ImprovOlympic.

Charna Halpern put Poehler and Fey together in an improv team. Before they met, Halpern told Poehler about Fey, saying she was like Poehler but with brown hair. Fey and Poehler began to take classes together and even began writing together.

Among their projects, Poehler and Fey workshopped a show called *Women of Color*. They wrote about fifteen minutes of material and then improvised the rest. Seth Meyers saw it and remembers there were not many people in the audience, but he knew he was watching people who were about to go on to something bigger. Poehler and Fey performed *Women of Color* only once.

The two women both auditioned for the Second City's touring company by performing different

Tina Fey met Poehler in Chicago when they were put together to form an improv team at ImprovOlympic. They became great friends while taking classes and writing sketches together.

characters. Both were accepted, and they traveled around the United States to various shows in a van. They didn't make much money, but they spent time together writing and working on performance skills, in addition to just enjoying time with other creative people. When Poehler returned to Chicago, she went back to improv class.

One of the classes she took at ImprovOlympic was with Family member Matt Besser. Besser was born and raised in Arkansas, and—Poehler noted—he dressed like a punk rock soccer player. He seemed fearless, and he paid great attention to detail when he performed. Besser asked her to join the newly created Upright Citizens Brigade (UCB) because the small group of males needed a woman. Poehler joined in 1996, and, working so closely with people she admired, she began to feel better about her skills. She started to really see herself as an artist.

The UCB regularly performed in Chicago and did showcases in New York and Los Angeles. Besser decided the now four-person group—including Ian Roberts and Matt Walsh—should leave Chicago to find something bigger. They gathered at a local diner and planned a move to New York as a group. "It's easier to be brave when you're not alone," Poehler notes in *Yes, Please*, explaining why they made

Matt Besser is a founding member of Upright Citizens Brigade. He still performs several times a week with UCB in Los Angeles.

the move, even though Poehler was in line to get a featured performer spot at the Second City and it would be hard to make it big as a group.

In April 1996, Poehler and friends packed up everything they owned and brought along her yellow Lab, Suki, for the trip to New York in a U-Haul truck. They didn't have an apartment or a job, but three years of learning from some of the best minds in Chicago improv taught Poehler that she could be anyone—and she could decide who she would be.

CHAPTER **FOUR**

Expanding Her Audience—and Mind—in New York

P oehler settled in New York City with boyfriend/ UCB founder Matt Besser, finding a street-level studio apartment at the crossroads of 10th Street and Bleecker Street in the city's artsy, bohemian, and (at the time) somewhat affordable Greenwich Village neighborhood. For decades, Greenwich Village and its residents have been known for nurturing creative minds and encouraging the expression of unconventional ideas. Most people refer to the neighborhood as "The Village."

The Village apartment had a view of garbage cans and bars on the windows—a common safety precaution for first-floor apartments in the city.

In 2013, the original members of UCB—(*left to right*) Ian Roberts, Amy Poehler, Matt Walsh, and Matt Besser—gathered in New York for an improv marathon in honor of their mentor Del Close.

Rats were another common issue. Once they caught on to this, Poehler and Besser put bowls over their oven burners to keep the rats from coming out of the walls and up through the oven. Still, for a creative twenty-six-year-old, it was all an adventure.

Getting Down to Business

A few minutes' walk uptown was Chelsea, another neighborhood that had a similar vibe. Poehler described the area as having an "underground downtown movement." It was in this area that UCB would perform at clubs, and years later they even opened their own theater.

UCB had performed in New York City once before moving there. The show was at a small West Village cabaret bar called Duplex. The performers were loud, had a lot of props, and didn't seem to fit in with other local acts. Now that they were New Yorkers themselves, they quickly booked a first show at a club called Surf Reality. They went on to guest-host weeknight shows at other venues, such as Luna Lounge.

At this point, UCB had evolved into a mixture of sketches and improvisation. They also made videotaped short films that they showed on giant monitors. They had two shows, *Millennium Approaches* and *Perestroika* (the Russian word for "openness," which is also the term for the mid-1980s political and social reform in Soviet Russia), that they had been working on back in Chicago. When not performing as herself, Poehler acted as a Girl Scout, an old man, or whatever the sketch called for.

UCB's motto is "Don't Think." The phrase was an improv direction given to them by their Chicago mentor, Del Close, and was also meant to represent the corporate world's mentality. "Don't Think" in improv means what it sounds like: get out of your head, stop planning, and let go—just do whatever comes naturally.

Besides being fun, every UCB show was a chance for the performers to get recognized by someone who could discover their talent. They would invite TV network executives to watch performances. But the shows were not a good way to make money, and it was hard to build an audience. Often they would put on masks and hand out flyers promoting their shows in Washington Square Park, near the New York University campus. At night, they would perform and write more.

Everything they did was necessary then to get attention. There were no YouTube or performance websites back then, so growing an audience was only by word of mouth. Still, comedians were doing well on TV. In the 1990s, Jerry Seinfeld and Rosanne Barr, among others, were not only finding success on TV talk shows but also getting their own sitcoms.

UCB was just one of many performance groups bent on performing their unique brand of comedy. The key was to stay true to their ideas and keep the creativity open.

Their second year in New York City, UCB found a place to perform in a small dance studio called Solo Arts. It was a five-story walk-up with an old, uneven floor. Poehler's brother, Greg, was living in the city, too, by now, and he became the studio's bartender. There, the group performed five nights a week and taught classes to pay rent. The night show, ASSSSCAT, was completely improvised. An audience suggestion would inspire a UCB member to perform a monologue, telling a story that the others onstage would act out.

When Poehler first moved to New York in 1996, she found work as a waitress (actually, now that she was working in a fancier place, she was called a "server") at Aquagrill. She moved on not too long after, as she and her fellow UCB performers supported themselves with odd jobs, writing work, and small TV appearances on shows such as *Late Night with Conan O'Brien*. In 1993, a young comedy writer named Conan O'Brien began hosting a late-night talk show on NBC that provided a lot of other young comedy writers and comedians with work—and cash. *Late Night with Conan O'Brien* offered $600 if a performer said more than six lines on the show.

The Gigs Start Getting Bigger

One character Poehler was hired to be was "Andy's Little Sister," wherein she played the sister of Conan's

CONAN O'BRIEN: A FRIEND TO COMEDY WRITERS

Once upon a time, Conan O'Brien was a comedy writer. The Massachusetts native was the third of six children born to a doctor/Harvard professor (his father, Thomas) and an attorney (his mother, Ruth). He attended Harvard University and became a writer and then president of the school's popular humor magazine, the *Harvard Lampoon*.

After graduation, O'Brien moved to Los Angeles, working as a comedy writer for an HBO comedy news show and performing with improv groups, such as the Groundlings. In 1988, he was hired as a writer for *SNL* and won an Emmy for his work that year. From 1991 to 1993, he served as a writer and producer of the most popular animated TV cartoon with an edge, *The Simpsons.*

He hosted his own late-night talk show, *Late Night with Conan O'Brien*, from 1993 to 2009. On June 1, 2009, he took over for comedian Jay Leno as host of *The Tonight Show*, NBC's legendary late show that aired one hour earlier and had a bigger, more mainstream audience. O'Brien's quirky show needed time to find its audience, so it was averaging fewer viewers than Leno had, and Leno started making NBC executives nervous by looking for a prime-time (8:00–11:00 p.m.) hosting job with other networks. NBC decided to ask Leno back,

(continued on the next page)

(continued from the previous page)

Conan O'Brien has helped give TV exposure to many of his talented friends, including Amy Poehler.

and O'Brien's last show was on January 22, 2010. He came back to late-night TV with *Conan*, a talk show on TBS, which debuted on November 8, 2010. In February 2015, O'Brien became the first American late-night talk show host to film his show in Cuba in more than fifty years, right after restrictions were loosened on Americans visiting that country.

sidekick, Andy Richter, who was obsessed with Conan. The show's writers would craft most of her lines, but Poehler's performance one night impressed two *SNL* cast members, Adam Sandler and Rob Schneider, who had been on set. They cast her in a role in the comedy film *Deuce Bigalow: Male Gigolo* (1999), in which a man becomes a gigolo after being mistaken for one while housesitting for a gigolo. It was her first big Hollywood role but not her first film as she had played "Woman Getting Squirted (with a hose)" in *Tomorrow Night*, a 1998 indie film by a fellow highly active creative mind, comedian/writer/director Louis C. K.

Poehler found more feature film work in *Wet Hot American Summer* (2001), a comedy about the last day at a summer camp for Jewish kids. But by then, UCB was getting plenty of attention.

Amy Poehler played Ruth, a woman with Tourette's syndrome, in *Deuce Bigalow: Male Gigolo*. The 1999 film starred *SNL* cast member Rob Schneider (*right*).

In 1998, the cable TV channel Comedy Central took notice of UCB's act. The continued encouragement by the group's manager, Dave Becky, to get executives to see the show had worked. They were offered a sketch show called *Upright Citizens Brigade*. It aired on Wednesday nights after another brand-new show, the animated comedy *South Park*, which quickly picked up a large audience—much larger than UCB's. Still, it was huge to be on TV. Poehler's parents hosted a viewing party in their basement, and her father got a UCB license plate soon after the first show aired.

The show's premise was that the UCB worked out of an underground bunker. Most episodes had a theme and the scenes were connected. Writing and planning for the TV show took up as much time as performing live, and Poehler's days were full, as UCB continued their work at Solo Arts. Although the TV show didn't gain a large audience, fans of the improv group found the TV show and vice versa. Poehler and Besser broke up while the show was

UPRIGHT CITIZENS BRIGADE KEEPS GROWING

UCB is still going strong. In 2005, UCB opened a theater in Los Angeles and moved into a larger theater in 2014. A year later, they opened a training center in New York, giving them space for an office and classrooms. Their needs grew, so in 2014 they opened a new center with fourteen classrooms.

UCB theaters produce an average of twenty-five shows a week for an audience price of less than $10. They launched UCBComedy.com in 2008, offering an even wider audience for their sketches and performers. Matt Besser, Matt Walsh, and Ian Roberts are still active UCB performers, and Poehler sometimes joins in shows.

in production, but they continued working together writing, producing, and performing.

With a larger audience thanks to TV, UCB found a bigger performance space at the old Harmony Theater on 22nd Street in Chelsea in 1999. It had been a burlesque house, covered in mirrors and small stages for the dancing girls, but Poehler and crew broke it all down themselves. Poehler also volunteered to clean the bathrooms. She spent New Year's Eve 1999 there and gathered there with friends after the terrorist attacks of September 11, 2001. In between, she performed in shows and fought over ideas. For a long time it was her second home.

After three years, the Comedy Central show ended in 2000. The city closed down the UCB's theater in 2002 because of safety issues the landlord had not taken care of. After taking time to think about how they would move forward, UCB found a 152-seat theater under a supermarket just a few blocks away on 26th Street. The theater is still there—and thriving—today.

CHAPTER FIVE

Ladies and Gentlemen, It's Saturday Night!

While Amy Poehler was in New York, building her résumé, she had many friends—some of whom she had performed with back in Chicago. Around the time Poehler moved to New York, Tina Fey did, too. While performing with Chicago's Second City in 1997, Fey had submitted several scripts for sketches to *SNL*'s head writer, Adam McKay, a former Second City performer. After meeting with *SNL* creator Lorne Michaels, she joined the show as a writer in 1997. In 1999, Fey became *SNL*'s first female head writer. In 2000, she began appearing in sketches, and she became a co-anchor on "Weekend Update," a humorous newscast of real events in the past week.

When Fey moved to New York, she connected with her Chicago friends and even joined UCB for some sketches. She began encouraging Poehler to consider auditioning for *SNL*, which Poehler finally did in 2001.

A Rough Start

Poehler was hired by *SNL* in August 2001. Her nervousness and excitement about the show and about turning thirty on September 16 were pushed aside temporarily on September 11, the day terrorists took over four passenger airplanes and flew two of them into the World Trade Center towers in lower Manhattan and one into the Pentagon in Arlington County, Virginia. The fourth plane went down near Shanksville, Pennsylvania, after passengers attempted to stop the hijackers. In all, almost three thousand people died.

On September 11, the cast had planned to have its first read-through of sketches they had been planning for the season opener. Yet the whole country was shaken up by the terror attacks. New York was especially hard hit, as fearless rescue and cleanup personnel took weeks to comb through the buildings' wreckage. "It was a tough time to join the show," Poehler explains in *Yes, Please*. "It felt like America might not ever smile, never mind laugh again."

Finally, it was decided that *SNL* must go on — people needed comedy. The September 29 show started with a short speech by New York mayor Rudy Giuliani, thanking police, firefighters, and other first responders. Paul Simon, a friend of *SNL* creator Lorne Michaels and a frequent guest over the show's long history, sang "The Boxer." Then the night's host, actress Reese Witherspoon, opened the show.

Poehler's first bit on camera was walking in the background of a talk show sketch called "Wake Up, Wakefield," but her parents noted that she couldn't be seen. A week later, in the final sketch of the night, there she was. It was a sketch she had written, in which she played a porn star on a date with actor Seann William Scott.

Poehler worried about staying at work on the show until a few episodes had passed. That's when a sketch she had written with cast member Will Ferrell, in which they played background actors, was approved to be on the show and got laughs. Feeling right at home, Poehler carved her name into the desk that cast members Molly Shannon before her and Kristen Wiig after her also carved their names into. She also felt fortunate to work with a cast full of strong female performers, including Rachel Dratch and Maya Rudolph, who would become her longtime friends.

Preparing for the Live Part of *SNL*

Backstage at *SNL* there was always a lot of joking and prank playing. Horatio Sanz, a castmate and

LORNE MICHAELS: *SNL'S* GODFATHER

There wouldn't be a *Saturday Night Live* without the guiding hand of Lorne Michaels. Michaels was born on November 17, 1940, in Toronto, Canada. He earned a degree in English from the University College at the University of Toronto and began as a writer for the Canadian Broadcasting Corporation's radio station.

Lorne Michaels, known for his deadpan humor, has helped launch the careers of many top comedy actors.

He moved to Los Angeles in 1968 and served as a writer for the popular TV sketch show *Laugh-In* before returning to Canada in the early 1970s to star in *The Hart and Lorne Terrific Comedy Hour* with Hart Pomerantz, a Canadian lawyer and TV personality. The show didn't last long, and by 1975 Michaels was in

(continued on the next page)

(continued from the previous page)

New York. He, along with NBC president Herb Schlosser and TV executive Dick Ebersol, created *Saturday Night Live*, which was meant to be a uniquely unpredictable sketch show performed in front of a live audience. Occasionally, Michaels even appears on *SNL* in a sketch, usually providing some deadpan humor.

Michaels is loyal to *SNL* cast members and has backed many of them in films and on TV, sometimes in roles based on popular *SNL* characters. He produced Tina Fey's TV sitcom *30 Rock* and popular film comedies, such as *Wayne's World* starring *SNL* stars Mike Meyers and Dana Carvey. Today, he continues to produce *The Tonight Show* and *Late Night*, starring former cast members Jimmy Fallon and Seth Meyers, respectively.

friend from back in Chicago's improv scene, would call her, pretending to be an odd gentleman named Gomez Vasquez Gomez. Another castmate, Chris Parnell, secretly hid under her desk for almost an hour as she wrote, hitting open her drawer from time to time.

There was also some crying, due in part to the built-up exhaustion of the show's production schedule and the anxiety that came with performing for millions. Poehler admits to crying sometimes when jokes she told didn't go as planned or she felt frustrated.

Members of the 2004 cast of *SNL* pose with Lorne Michaels and comedian Steve Martin. From left: Seth Meyers, Poehler, Fey, Maya Rudolph, Michaels, Martin, Fred Armisen, Will Forte, Rachel Dratch, and Horatio Sanz.

SNL's weekly schedule is well known as being tough for writers, cast members, and hosts alike. Typically, a free-form cast meeting is held on the Monday before a show. There, everyone—including the producers and Lorne Michaels—gathers to suggest ideas for sketches. Some writing may occur, but usually that is saved for Tuesday, when writers often write and revise into the next morning. At 5:00 p.m. on Wednesday, sketches are read aloud as makeup artists, costumers, prop artists, and others help plan how each sketch will look. The sketches have not been narrowed down at this point so there may be many more discussed than will ever air on TV. After the read-through, Michaels gathers with the host, head writer, and producers to figure out which sketches should be finalized for the show. Cast members and writers learn the next day whether their work has been accepted or must be rewritten by looking at a printed packet of accepted sketches. Rehearsals begin late on Thursday or Friday. The cast performs a full show rehearsal onstage for an audience at 8:00 p.m. (EST) on Saturday night, and then the show goes live at 11:32 p.m.

Poehler was somewhat used to the hectic energy that went with live performing, thanks to her improv background. And her work was appreciated at *SNL*. In January 2002, she went from her starting position as a featured player to a genuine cast member. She was only the third person to go from featured player to cast member in one season.

In her seven years on *SNL*, Poehler wasn't afraid to speak up to support ideas in which she believed. From time to time, she had to draw the line with writers and cast members and let them know what she would and wouldn't do. "Amy made it clear that she wasn't there to be cute," remembers Tina Fey in her 2011 book, *Bossypants*. "She wasn't there to play wives and girlfriends in the boys' scenes. She

was there to do what she wanted and she did not...
care if you liked it."

Poehler continued performing with UCB, even
while on *SNL*. Her roles on *SNL* were as diverse as
they were when she performed improv in a theater
for a small audience. She was not afraid to perform
as popular celebrities, including a white-skinned,
playful Michael Jackson. She also was equally
unafraid to take on challenging noncelebrity roles,
like a trashy one-legged farting girl named Amber or
frequent Appalachian Emergency Room patient Netti
Bo Dance. Her mother's favorite impression was
her Hillary Clinton. At the time, beginning around
2007, then–New York senator Clinton was attempt-
ing to win the Democratic nomination for president.
Poehler's Hillary was self-assured, laughed hardily,
and was ultimately irritated by the ease with which
Republican vice presidential candidate and former
Alaska governor Sarah Palin (played by Tina Fey)
slid into the nomination.

Fey and Poehler won raves for their comedic
portrayals of the gutsy but clueless governor and
the woman who wanted nothing more than her own
time in the White House. They were so popular that
the real Sarah Palin and Hillary Clinton each made
appearances on the show with the actresses. The
senator, who visited the set soon after Poehler
learned she was pregnant, was a good sport and

Fey and Poehler, shown hosting the Golden Globe Awards in 2015, are longtime friends who are often paired together. They became household names while poking fun at real-life politicians on *SNL*.

asked Poehler on camera, "Do I really laugh like that?"

In 2004, Poehler made *SNL* history when she joined Tina Fey behind the "Weekend Update" anchor desk. They were the first all-female *SNL* news team. According to Fey, she made it happen fast—without Michael's consent. And the choice was a good one. The pairing, wrote *Chicago Times* reporter Rachel Sklar, "has been a hilarious, pitch-perfect success as they play off each other with quick one-liners and deadpan delivery." The two women were a hit and their chemistry was obvious, even though most viewers didn't know their long improv history and how long it took to climb into those chairs.

CHAPTER
SIX

Getting Personal

W hen Tina Fey left *SNL* after the 2005–2006 season, Poehler was joined on "Weekend Update" by castmate Seth Meyers, whom she had first met in the Chicago improv scene. The ease of seeing two friends ping-pong stories and comments back and forth was enjoyable for the audience and the castmates, who became even better friends.

Politics and Comedy

The 2008–2009 season opened on September 13 with the return of Fey, performing as Sarah Palin. She and Poehler, as Hillary Clinton, provided "A Nonpartisan Message from Governor Sarah Palin & Senator Hillary Clinton." The sketch, written by Meyers with jokes added by Poehler, Fey, and

Friends since meeting in Chicago's improv scene in the 1990s, Poehler and Seth Meyers have stayed close. In 2015, they both premiered comedy series on the online streaming subscription service Hulu.

SNL producer Mike Shoemaker, featured the two women comparing themselves and discussing the sexism in the 2008 presidential campaign. As "Sarah Palin" tries to present herself as the candidate for the job, "Hillary Clinton" gets more and more irritated by the former governor's sudden rise to fame—and possibly the vice presidency—as Republican candidate John McCain's running mate.

The sketch was a hit with the media and fans alike, as Palin's line "I can see Russia from my house" became a running joke even for political pundits discussing the upcoming elections that November. Many critics pointed out that people were hoping *SNL* would tackle the public fascination with

Poehler's Hillary Clinton wig and blue suit, along with Fey's Sarah Palin costume, were displayed with other costumes during *SNL*'s fortieth anniversary celebration in 2015.

Governor Palin, and *SNL* did just that. Senator McCain's advisor Carly Fiorina was not as happy, claiming that the "disrespectful in the extreme" sketch showed Senator Clinton as being "very substantive," but Palin was portrayed as "totally superficial." It was clear by now that just by poking fun at politics, *SNL* had a hand in how people viewed candidates.

Three days later it was announced that Poehler would be leaving *SNL* after the birth of her first child. Poehler had married Canadian actor Will Arnett on August 29, 2003. Arnett, who is best known for his roles as George Oscar Bluth II ("G.O.B.") in the TV comedy *Arrested Development* (2003–2006 on FOX; 2013 on Netflix) and Devon Banks on Tina Fey's TV comedy *30 Rock* (2008), creatively paired with Poehler numerous times, including four episodes of *Arrested Development* and the 2007 Will Ferrell comedy film *Blades of Glory*, in which they played a brother and sister ice-skating pair who were a little too close for comfort.

It was while nine months pregnant that Poehler gave one of her most memorable *SNL* performances, with fourteen million people watching. Governor Palin was appearing on the show in one sketch, and on the Friday night before the show was to air, producer Lorne Michaels suggested Poehler, Meyers, and the other news writers craft a spot for her in the "Weekend Update" segment. Amy suggested they could have Palin perform a rap, and then someone pointed out that Poehler could do the rap after the Alaskan governor suddenly turns shy.

As Meyers remembered it, "Amy's eyes went wide with glee and she left the room with a notebook in hand." Soon, after Meyers and castmate Andy Samberg added jokes, she had a sketch written. It involved other castmates taking part in the rap while in moose and Eskimo suits.

In the segment, Palin excuses herself from the rap, and Meyers asks Poehler if she could do the rap. She acts hesitant and says she kind of knows it. She then looks into the camera and in a deep voice counts, "One, two, three." The music starts, and heavily pregnant Poehler, in a pantsuit, pushes up from behind the desk to rap. "My name is Sarah Palin and you all know me, vice prezy nominee of the G.O.P. Gonna need your vote in the next election. Can I get a 'what? what?' from the senior section…"

"In my opinion," notes Tina Fey in *Bossypants*, "the most meaningful moment for women in the 2008 campaign was not Governor Palin's convention speech or Hillary Clinton conceding her 1,896 delegates. The moment most emblematic of how things have changed for women in America was nine-months-pregnant Amy Poehler rapping as Sarah Palin and tearing the roof off the place."

A New Role: Mom

The following week Poehler prepared for the next show, as usual, except that her baby had other ideas. After a Friday dress rehearsal that lasted until midnight, everyone went home. Poehler sent Meyers a text message at about 3:30 a.m. to tell him her water broke—and he'd be great on "Weekend Update" without her.

The birth had one major complication, but not the medical kind. Poehler's obstetrician/gynecologist was a wonderful, elderly Italian man who had delivered elegant actress Sophia Loren's children forty years prior. He was kind, encouraging, and supportive right up until he had a heart attack in his sleep and died the day before Poehler went into labor.

Poehler ended up needing a C-section. Son Archie was born on Saturday, October 25, at 6:09 p.m. Poehler watched *SNL* that night, as Meyers started the update by saying, "I'm Seth Meyers. Amy Poehler is not here because she's having a baby," which made the audience loudly cheer. Then *SNL* friends Maya Rudolph and Kenan Thompson sang a duet version of Frankie Valli's "Can't Take My Eyes Off You," subbing the chorus of "Oh pretty baby!" with "We love you, Amy!"

Poehler returned to *SNL* after her pregnancy on December 6, 2008, and performed in two more

Amy Poehler holds her son Archie in October 2009. She has no problem telling women that she gets so much work done because she is lucky to have great child care help from nannies and her ex-husband, Will Arnett.

shows before saying good-bye. She has also returned several times since. While pregnant with her second son, Abel (born August 6, 2010), she returned for an *SNL* Mother's Day show in May 2010. She also came back as host of the show for its 2010 season opener on September 25, and then returned again that year in November as part of *SNL*'s special "The Women of *SNL*." In 2015, she returned for *SNL's* fortieth anniversary show, where she anchored "Weekend Update" with Tina Fey and the show's first female newscaster, Jane Curtain.

JANE CURTAIN: WEEKEND UPDATE'S FIRST LADY

Jane Curtain's most memorable *SNL* work, including her time as the first female anchor of "Weekend Update," was accented by her deadpan humor. Born on September 6, 1947, in Cambridge, Massachusetts, Curtain was part of *SNL*'s original cast. After graduating with an associate's degree from Elizabeth Seton Junior College and spending one year at Northwestern University, she dropped out to perform as a comedic actress. She joined the group the Proposition, working with them until 1972, and then starred in an off-Broadway play before joining *SNL*.

SNL actress Jane Curtain and actor Dan Aykroyd perform as Prymaat and Beldar, the married couple in the classic *SNL* sketch "The Coneheads."

On *SNL*, she often played serious, straight-laced characters, which were a bit like herself at the time. She didn't quite fit in with the wild, male-dominated original *SNL* cast, which then included Gilda Radner as well as Bill Murray, John Belushi, and Dan Aykroyd. Her most famous work on the show besides "Weekend Update" was as Prymaat, wife and mother in the Conehead family. This role was later reprised in the movie *Coneheads* (1993) and more recently in TV ads for State Farm insurance.

She later won two Emmys for Lead Actress in a Comedy for her work on the TV sitcom *Kate and Allie* (1984–1989). Another popular role for her was Dr. Mary Albright on the sitcom *3rd Rock from the Sun* (1996–2001). She continues to act on TV and in films, including in *The Heat,* a 2013 comedy starring Melissa McCarthy and Sandra Bullock.

69

Even while away from *SNL*, Poehler has always stayed busy creatively. She and Fey found great success with the films *Mean Girls* and *Baby Mama*. In *Mean Girls,* written by Fey, Poehler plays the "cool mom" of obnoxious schoolgirl Regina George (Rachel McAdams). The 2004 film opened at number one at the U.S. box office and grossed more than $129 million worldwide. *Baby Mama* has Poehler playing a troublemaking surrogate mother for Fey's single businesswoman character. That 2008 film also went to number one in its first week. Even after some not-so-stellar reviews, it made a very healthy $64,163,648.

Poehler, who is so open about so many things, has mostly kept one painful thing out of public view: her divorce from Will Arnett. After nine years of marriage, they announced they were separating in September 2012. The couple, who did so much creative work together, have done a good job of managing their split and helping their kids handle it. "Will and I are very, very good friends," she told radio host Howard Stern on his show in October 2014. "We are doing a really good job. I don't think a ten-year marriage constitutes a failure. I think relationships are really tough."

CHAPTER **SEVEN**

This Mother's Work Is Never Done

Even though her days as a cast member on *SNL* are over, Poehler has continued to be as creative as ever. Her work is also more diverse than ever, and she has more flexibility with her time as she raises her two young sons.

She found herself with another hit on her hands in 2009. After a rocky first season, her sitcom *Parks and Recreation* found an audience even after being shelved for half a season in fall 2010. As obsessively organized Leslie Knope, assistant parks director of Pawnee, Indiana, Poehler was "trying to play someone who—even though she's kind of grade-A bananas—could maybe exist in the world," she told *Glamour* magazine in 2011. Poehler led an ensemble cast that included Aziz Ansari, Nick Offerman, Rashida

Poehler and two *Parks and Recreation* costars, Aziz Ansari (*left*) and Chris Pratt, attend a panel discussion promoting the show. They had great chemistry on screen and off.

Jones, Chris Pratt, Aubrey Plaza, Paul Schneider, Adam Scott, and Rob Lowe.

When her parents visited the set, they were happy to hear how nice Poehler is to everyone. "Our biggest thrill is hearing how much the crew, from the girl who cleans the trailer to the driver to the director, like working with Amy," her mother told the *Wall Street Journal* in 2011.

Starting the show was tough for Poehler, who filmed in Los Angeles. At the time, her first-born son was only a few months old. She felt guilty for working but knew she wanted to work because she enjoyed the creative outlet. Still, the regular hours of TV were more stable than *SNL*'s schedule, and she

Poehler, pictured at the Golden Globes, tries to have fun at stuffy award shows—whether she is nominated or hosting. Sometimes that means planning something beforehand.

had time to write or cowrite some episodes. She was proud of the show's writing and the talented cast and often called it her dream job, saying she was in a lead role on a show she would actually watch.

All In at Award Shows

Poehler's comedic timing and acting on *Parks and Recreation* were awarded with four Emmy nominations (2010–2014) and three Golden Globe nominations (2012–2014). She won the Golden Globe for Best Actress in a Comedy Series—TV or Musical in 2014. Her nomination was also a great performance—with U2 lead singer Bono. As her name was read with the other nominees, Poehler was shown at Bono's table, working out her nerves by taking deep breaths as Bono rubbed her shoulders. When her name was called as the winner, Poehler turned to give Bono a celebratory kiss, but it quickly turned into a one-sided make-out session, much to Bono's surprise—and the audience's delight.

Poehler had earned that 2014 Golden Globe, not just for her role as Leslie Knope, but also as a much-anticipated co-host of the Globes for three years (2013–2015) alongside Tina Fey. The Globes signed Poehler and Fey to a three-year contract, which was a testament to their popularity, amazing success and chemistry, and ability to think on their feet to make a large and varied audience laugh.

LOSING AN AWARD IS NEVER AWKWARD FOR POEHLER

Anyone who is cool likes to pretend that awards don't matter, but anyone who is honest will admit that winning one is awesome. Poehler is both cool and honest. So, to combat the awkwardness of being excited to be nominated but then not winning and having to act like it's no big deal, Poehler decided to distract herself as the nominees are announced. She has become good at controlling that moment, if only in her mind.

The first time she was nominated was for an Emmy in the Outstanding Supporting Actress in a Comedy category, for *SNL*, in 2008. She collected crazy glasses and even an eye patch and easily got her fellow nominees—Kristen Chenoweth, Jane Krakowski, Elizabeth Perkins, Kristen Wiig, and Vanessa Williams—to join her in the fun while Wiig won.

In 2011, she encouraged her fellow nominees in the Lead Actress in a Comedy category—Edie Falco, Tina Fey, Laura Linney, and Melissa McCarthy—to act as if they were in a beauty contest. As each name was called, the actress would excitedly run up onstage. There, they held hands in a mixture of mock and real anticipation. McCarthy was then given roses and a crown when she won.

Sometimes, though, what makes some people laugh offends others. The Golden Globes are considered one of the looser and more fun award shows, in part because guests are seated at tables, often drinking. For this reason, hosts tend to tease Hollywood stars, including those sitting right in front of them, waiting to win awards. In their first year as hosts, Poehler and Fey made a joke about singer Taylor Swift and her reputation for being a serial dater of young men. Swift was there that night and was not amused. When later asked about it in a *Vanity Fair* article, the then–twenty-three year-old singer repeated a quote originally said by former U.S. secretary of state Madeline Albright: "There's a special place in hell for women who don't help other women." Both Fey and Poehler expressed surprise that Swift was so upset but kept their senses of humor intact. "I feel bad if she was upset," Poehler told the *Hollywood Reporter*. "I am a feminist, and she is a young and talented girl. That being said, I do agree I am going to hell, but for other reasons—mostly boring tax stuff."

Looking to Help Others

Poehler isn't just all talk when it comes to being a feminist. She is careful of the image she portrays to women—and eager to be honest. She is open about how she manages to appear to have it all—by not doing all the work herself. She praises her children's nanny and makes it clear that it's difficult to have children and work hard without help. Poehler also discusses her looks in a frank manner in her book, *Yes, Please*. She details her physical likes and dislikes about herself (in short, she loves her butt, is not so happy with her legs, and thinks her smile is sometimes a little crazy). It's this honesty that makes Poehler not only a great writer but a relatable person, especially for young people who feel unsure about themselves, their abilities, and their looks. "If you are lucky, there is a moment in your life when you have some say as to what your currency is going to be. I decided early on it was not going to be my looks," Poehler writes. "Decide what your currency is early. Let go of what you will never have."

Poehler's eagerness to put people at ease with themselves is why she and friends Meredith Wilson and Amy Miles created Smart Girls at the Party. They began in fall 2008 with a web series, intended to "help girls find confidence in their own aspirations and talents." It is meant to combat all of the negative messages that are everywhere online, and its outlets on social media are safe places where young women can be heard and offered a response. Through the organization's "Call to Action" campaigns, young people are encouraged to volunteer, be more involved in the world around them, and expand their worldview.

As part of their Smart Girls web series, Poehler and friends interview girls who are uniquely talented or have a fresh point of view. And at the end of every episode, they have a spontaneous dance party. Since 2012, Smart Girls has had its own YouTube channel focused on the same message. Within two years, it quickly amassed five million video views, which encouraged Legendary Entertainment to buy it and expand on the organization's reach and financial power in 2014. On Facebook, the organization regularly promotes the positive actions of young women to its half a million followers, and it does the same to its 120,000 followers on Twitter.

Another of Poehler's projects aimed to help others is her role as an ambassador with the nonprofit organization Worldwide Orphans Foundation. She has been a part of the WWO since 2013, when she traveled with pediatrician (and CEO of WWO) Jane Aronson and WWO staffers to Haiti, which had an increase in the already large number of orphans and homeless since the devastating 2010 earthquake that killed more than one hundred thousand people and destroyed thousands of buildings, further hindering the small country's issues with poverty and poor housing conditions. Poehler supports WWO by helping to raise awareness of its mission to

DR. JANE ARONSON: PROTECTOR OF ORPHANS

Poehler found a friend in Dr. Jane Aronson, a pediatrician and infectious disease specialist who passionately dedicates herself to helping orphans around the world. She was born November 10, 1951, in Brooklyn, New York, and grew up in nearby Long Island. After graduating from college, she became a teacher for ten years until she earned a doctor of osteopathic medicine degree.

After a series of high-level jobs in the fields of pediatric medicine and infectious diseases, she founded Worldwide Orphans Foundation in 1997. Its mission is to "transform

In 2015, Poehler was honored for her charity work at the unite4:humanity ceremony, which awards entertainers who highlight great causes. Worldwide Orphans CEO and president Dr. Jane Aronson (*right*) presented her award.

the lives of orphaned children to help them become healthy, independent, productive members of their communities and the world." It has major programs in Bulgaria, Ethiopia, Vietnam, Serbia, and Haiti.

The doctor has visited numerous orphanages in Asia, Africa, eastern Europe, Russia, and Latin America. She lives in New York with her sons Desalegn, who was adopted from Ethiopia, and Ben, adopted from Vietnam.

transform the lives of orphans. She also raises critical funds to support WWO programming across the globe by hosting galas, taking part in speeches and events, and contributing financially on her own and through special shows with Upright Citizens Brigade.

The trip to Haiti was a game-changer for Poehler. She flew there on New Year's Day 2013. At the time of the trip, Haiti had more than seven hundred orphanages with more than 430,000 orphans. The streets were filled with chaos, and the orphanages were filled with children eager for hugs and in need of help. Back home in New York before the trip, Poehler's mind had been filled with heartbroken thoughts about the end of her marriage and how difficult the divorce would be on her sons. By the end of the trip, she realized how lucky her life is—and how her kids' lives are lucky, too.

Poehler has been in a relationship with fellow comedic actor Nick Kroll, a stand-up comedian and star of his own Comedy Central show, since 2013. True to many of her past relationships, they started as friends.

Moving On

In 2015, Poehler and Fey finished work on their third film together, *Sisters*, written by longtime *SNL* writer Paula Pell. In it, sisters enjoy one last house party before their parents sell their home. *SNL* stars Maya Rudolph, Kate McKinnon, and Bobby Moynihan have feature roles. Poehler also joined the cast of *Wet Hot American Summer: First Day of Camp*, a prequel to the 2001 film that was released on Netflix.

Poehler is eager to produce and direct more. In 2014, she took on the task of co-executive-producing the short-lived TV sitcom *Welcome to Sweden*, along with her brother, Greg, who wrote, starred in, and produced the show with his sister. It was based on his life as an American living in Sweden with his Swedish-born wife and three kids.

Now that Poehler has the ability to take the lead on developing new projects, she is eager to give women in comedy more attention. Since 2014, she has served as executive producer on *Broad City*, the Comedy Central sitcom developed from a web series by the show's stars, Ilana Glazer and Abbi Jacobson.

Poehler stays practical about her power in making things happen. "Power sometimes comes down to knowing the vocabulary, figuring out how the system works and how to work within it," she explained in a 2014 *Elle* interview.

Mostly, Amy Poehler just wants to keep creating, trying new things, and bringing new talent and ideas into the light for audiences to enjoy. "I like to do things that challenge me and make me nervous," she said in *Elle*. "You learn early as an actor that creating your own material is the only way to have any control. Hollywood is like a bad boyfriend. You can't stand around and wait to be asked to dance."

Fact Sheet ON AMY POEHLER

Birthplace: Newton, Massachusetts

Birthdate: September 16, 1971

Birth Order: Older of two children

Current Residence: New York City and Los Angeles

College Attended: Boston College

First Paying Performance: In 1998, she had a one-time role on the Michael J. Fox sitcom *Spin City* and appeared in sketches on the late-night talk show *Late Night with Conan O'Brien.*

First Film Appearance: *Tomorrow Night* in 1998

Family: Parents Bill and Eileen are both former teachers. Eileen has served as an elementary school and special education teacher. Bill later worked as a financial planner. Her brother, Greg, is three years younger and is now an actor and writer. She has two sons, Archie and Abel, from her past marriage to actor Will Arnett.

Fact Sheet ON AMY POEHLER'S WORK

Famous Mentors/Major Influences
Carol Burnett, Gilda Radner, Del Close

Membership in Important Troupes
Upright Citizens Brigade (1996–2001)

Breakthrough Life Performances
Saturday Night Live (beginning in 2001)

Television Appearances and Series
Spin City (one episode, 1998)
Late Night with Conan O'Brien (select episodes, 1998)
Upright Citizens Brigade (1998–2000)
Undeclared (select episodes, 2002)
Arrested Development (select episodes, 2004–2005)
SpongeBob SquarePants (animated/one episode, 2005)
The Simpsons (animated/select episodes, 2005, 2014)
O'Grady (animated/one episode, 2006)
Wonder Showzen (select episodes, 2006)
Saturday Night Live (2001–2008; select episodes 2009–2012)
The Mighty B! (animated, 2008–2011)
Parks and Recreation (2009–2015)
30 Rock (one episode, 2012)
Louie (one episode, 2012)

Broad City (select episodes, 2011, 2014)
Welcome to Sweden (select episodes, 2014)
The Awesomes (animated, 2014)
Kroll Show (select episodes, 2014–2015)
Saturday Night Live: 40th Anniversary Show (2015)
Wet Hot American Summer: First Day of Camp (2015)

Film Appearances

Tomorrow Night (1998)
Deuce Bigalow: Male Gigolo (1999)
Wet Hot American Summer (2001)
Martin & Orloff (2002)
Shortcut to Happiness (2004)
Mean Girls (2004)
Envy (2004)
Southland Tales (2006)
Tenacious D in the Pick of Destiny (2006)
The Ex (2006)
Blades of Glory (2007)
On Broadway (2007)
Shrek the Third (animated, 2007)
Mr. Woodcock (2007)
Wild Girls Gone (2007)
Hamlet 2 (2008)
Horton Hears a Who! (animated, 2008)

Baby Mama (2008)
Spring Breakdown (2009)
Alvin and the Chipmunks: The Squeakquel (animated, 2009)
Monsters vs. Aliens (animated, 2009)
Freak Dance (2010)
Hoodwinked Too! Hood vs. Evil (2011)
Alvin and the Chipmunks: Chipwrecked (animated, 2011)
They Came Together (2014)
Inside Out (animated, 2015)
Sisters (2015)

Books Written
Yes, Please (2014)

Writer Credits
Escape from It's a Wonderful Life (1996)
Upright Citizens Brigade (1998–2000)
Soundtracks Live (2004)
ASSSSCAT: Improv (2005)
Wild Girls Gone (2007)
The Mighty B! (2008–2011)
UCB Comedy Originals (one episode, 2013)
70th Golden Globe Awards (2013)

Old Soul (2014)
71st Golden Globe Awards (2014)
72nd Golden Globe Awards (2015)
Parks and Recreation (select episodes, 2010–2015)

Director Credits
Parks and Recreation (three episodes, 2012, 2013,
    2015)
Broad City (2014)

Producer Credits
ASSSSCAT: Improv (TV film, 2005)
Wild Girls Gone (film, 2007)
The Mighty B! (TV, 2008–2011)
Old Soul (TV film, 2014)
Welcome to Sweden (TV, 2014)
Parks and Recreation (TV, 2009–2015)
Broad City (TV, 2014–2015)
Difficult People (TV, 2015)
Sisters (film, 2015)

Awards Won
Golden Globe for Best Performance by an Actress in
    a Television Series—Comedy or Musical on *Parks
    and Recreation* (2014)
American Comedy Award for Best Comedy Actress—
    TV on *Parks and Recreation* (2014)

Critics Choice TV Award for Best Actress in a
Comedy Series on *Parks and Recreation* (2012)
Gracie Allen Award for Outstanding Female Actor in
a Leading Role in a Comedy Series on *Parks and
Recreation* (2013)
MTV Movie Award for Best WTF Moment in *Baby
Mama* (2008)
Writers Guild of America award for Comedy/Variety—
Music, Awards, Tributes—Specials on the 71st
Golden Globe Awards (2015)

Critical Reviews

"As Leslie Knope on *'Parks and Recreation,'* as a *'Saturday Night Live'* cast member, and as a trustworthy awards-show iconoclast, Amy Poehler has helped define comedy in the past decade and a half, pushing it forward, making it more interesting, more feminist, better. Her particular genius has much to do with confidence and how she deploys it: she wins us over with warmth, self-assurance, and energy, and she satirizes fair targets intelligently."
—Sarah Larson, the *New Yorker*

"Lovely, brilliant and utterly fearless, [Poehler and Fey] made awards-show hosting an art form again, helming three hours of occasionally hilarious, occasionally emotional and surprisingly enjoyable TV."
—Mary McNamara, *Los Angeles Times,* on the 2013 Golden Globes

"[Poehler and Fey] killed it last year with their opening monologue and they did so again this year."
—Gilbert Cruz, *New York* magazine, on the 2014 Golden Globes

"Ms. Poehler's slow drip of gripes ("Dear Lord, when will I finish this book?") breaks Rule No. 1 about comedy and about writing: Never let them see you sweat."—Dwight Gardner, *New York Review of Books* on *Yes, Please.*

"*Yes, Please* arrives on printed pages sandwiched between cardboard covers and is currently lodged in the No 2 spot of the *New York Times* bestsellers list, so technically, yes: it is a book. However, it's the type of title the publishing business sometimes refers to as a 'non-book,' meaning that it has few of the qualities bookish people like to think of as exemplifying the form."—Laura Miller, the *Guardian* on *Yes, Please*.

"Tina Fey and Amy Poehler left no superstar unscathed during their riotous opening monologue at the 72nd Golden Globe Awards, which opened with Fey delivering the warmest of introductions: 'Good evening, good evening, and welcome you bunch of despicable, spoiled, minimally talented brats.'"—Jon Blistein, *Rolling Stone,* on the 2015 Golden Globes

"Let us now praise '*Parks and Recreation,*' which ends Tuesday night in an effervescence of heart and hope, proof positive that success and significance are not always measured in gold, statuary or otherwise."—Mary McNamara, *Los Angeles Times,* on the finale of *Parks and Recreation*

Timeline

1971 Amy Meredith Poehler is born to Eileen and Bill Poehler in Newton, Massachusetts, on September 16.

1974 Brother Greg is born on October 11.

1975 *Saturday Night Live* premieres on NBC on October 11 with a cast that features Gilda Radner, Jane Curtin, Laraine Newman, Bill Murray, John Belushi, Dan Aykroyd, Chevy Chase, and Garrett Morris.

1976 The Poehler family moves to Burlington, Massachusetts.

1987 Amy gets her first job as a junior secretary in a podiatrist's office.

1989 Graduates high school and attends Boston College in the fall; sees My Mother's Fleabag improv troupe.

1993 Graduates college and moves to Chicago with friends.

1993–1996 Joins ImprovOlympic (iO) and the Second City for classes and performances; teams up with Upright Citizens Brigade; meets Tina Fey and Seth Meyers, among other longtime friends.

1996 Moves to New York with UCB, including boyfriend Matt Besser in April.

1997 Tina Fey joins *Saturday Night Live.*

1998 *Upright Citizens Brigade* begins airing on Comedy Central; Poehler appears on *Late Night with Conan O'Brien* and the sitcom *Spin City.*

1999 UCB sets up in the old Harmony Theater on 22nd Street in Chelsea; Tina Fey becomes head writer on *SNL*; *Deuce Bigelow: Male Gigolo* is released.

2000 UCB's Comedy Central show is canceled; Tina Fey becomes an anchor on *SNL's* "Weekend Update."

2001 *Wet Hot American Summer* (the film) is released. Poehler auditions for *SNL* and is hired as a featured player; she appears briefly in the season opener on September 29; on October 6, she is featured in a sketch she wrote.

2002 Becomes an *SNL* cast member; UCB's 22nd Street theater closes in New York City; they find a new theater on 26th Street.

August 29, 2003 Marries Will Arnett.

2004 Joins *SNL's* "Weekend Update," with coanchor Tina Fey; *Mean Girls* is released.

2005 Is joined by Seth Meyers at the "Weekend Update" desk after Fey leaves *SNL*; UCB opens a theater in Los Angeles.

2006 UCB opens a training center in New York City.

2007 *Blades of Glory* is released.

2008 *Baby Mama* is released; the Smart Girls at the Party web series begins. Poehler portrays senator/Democratic presidential candidate Hillary Clinton alongside Tina Fey as Alaska governor/Republican vice presidential candidate Sarah

Palin in one of her most famous *SNL* sketches, "A Nonpartisan Message from Governor Sarah Palin & Senator Hillary Clinton." On October 25, she gives birth to son Archie. She ends her time as an *SNL* cast member soon after.

2009 *Parks and Recreation* begins airing on NBC.

2010 Hosts the *SNL* season opener; comes back to *SNL* for a Mother's Day special and a November "Women of *SNL*" special; gives birth to son Abel on August 6.

September 2012 Announces separation from Will Arnett; they divorce in 2014.

2013 Travels to Haiti with the nonprofit organization Worldwide Orphans Foundation to visit orphanages; hosts the 70th Golden Globes with Tina Fey; begins a relationship with Nick Kroll.

2014 Wins a Golden Globe for Best Actress in a Comedy Series—TV or Musical; hosts the 71st Golden Globes with Tina Fey; *Welcome to Sweden* and *Broad City* premiere; her book, *Yes, Please*, is released.

2015 Hosts the 72nd Golden Globes with Tina Fey; appears on *SNL*'s fortieth anniversary show; episodes of *Wet Hot American Summer: First Day of Camp* air on Netflix; *Sisters* is released.

Glossary

accent A way of talking shared by a group (as the people of a country or region).

anesthesia Loss of bodily sensation with or without loss of consciousness through use of drugs.

contractions Movements of muscles in the womb when a woman is giving birth to a child.

C-section Cesarean section; a surgical operation for giving birth in which a cut is made in the mother's abdomen so that the baby can be removed through the opening.

episode A television show, radio show, etc., that is one part of a series.

feisty Not afraid to fight or argue; very lively and aggressive.

feminist A person who believes that men and women should have equal rights and opportunities.

frantic Feeling or showing a lot of fear and worry.

gynecologist A doctor who deals with the diseases and routine physical care of the reproductive system of women.

immerse To become fully involved in some activity or interest.

improvisation (improv) The act of speaking or performing without preparation.

inspiration A force or influence that makes someone want to do something or that gives someone an idea about what to do or create.

obstetrician A doctor who specializes in human
     births and the medical needs of a woman
     before and after them.

outgoing A description for someone who is friendly
     and likes being with and talking to other people.

pageant A play or performance made of scenes
     from a historical or meaningful event or a
     legend.

parody A piece of writing, music, or art that imitates
     the style of someone or something else in a
     funny way.

podiatrist A doctor who specializes in the care and
     treatment of the human foot.

producer A person in charge of making and provid-
     ing the money for a play, movie, record, or other
     creation.

recite To read something out loud or say something
     from memory, usually for an audience.

rehearsal An event at which a person or group
     practices an activity (such as singing, dancing,
     or acting) to prepare for a public performance.

remortgage The process of paying off one mort-
     gage with the proceeds from a new mortgage
     using the same property as security; also called
     refinancing.

sketch A short, funny performance.

sitcom A show that is on television regularly and is
     about a group of characters who are involved in
     different funny situations.

troupe A group of actors, singers, or performers who work together.

unconventional Not based on or conforming to what is generally done or believed.

vaudeville A type of entertainment popular chiefly in the United States in the early twentieth century, featuring a mixture of specialty acts such as burlesque comedy and song and dance.

workshop A series of classes or meetings in which a small group of people learn the skills used in doing something.

For More Information

Canadian Improv Games
135 Séraphin-Marion
Ottawa, ON K1N 6N5
Canada
Website: http://improv.ca
This organization brings high school students from across Canada together to explore the art of improv in a supportive and fun environment.

ImprovOlympic (iO), Chicago
1501 N. Kingsbury Street
Chicago, IL
(312) 929-2401
Website: http://ioimprov.com/chicago
Enjoy improv at the theater where Poehler met Tina Fey! Classes offered here include those on writing and musical improv, and the theater's founder Charna Halpern still teaches here.

NBC Studio Tour
30 Rockefeller Plaza
New York, NY
(212) 664-3056
Website: http://www.nbc.com/tickets-and-nbc-studio-tour#tour
Take a guided tour of NBC's halls and studios, including Studio 8H, where *Saturday Night Live's* stars do their thing! Information about tickets to future *SNL* rehearsals and live

performances can also be found at the same website.

The Paley Center (formerly the Museum of Television and Radio)
25 West 52nd Street
New York, NY 10019
Website: http://mediaorigin.paleycenter.org
The Paley Center's New York City and Beverly Hills, California, locations both feature screenings of popular TV shows from the past (including The *Carol Burnett Show* and *Saturday Night Live*), conversations with current TV and media stars, and private consoles for you to watch old TV shows and past museum interviews that you select. Catch a conversation with the cast of *Parks and Recreation* in its archive.

The Second City, Toronto (main stage)
51 Mercer Street
Toronto M5V 9G9
Canada
(416) 343-0011
Website: http://www.secondcity.com/shows/toronto
The venerable Second City franchise has improv stages in Toronto, Chicago, and Hollywood. In Toronto, kids can get into the act and learn about improv after watching shows at the John Candy Box Theatre.

Upright Citizens Brigade, Chelsea
307 W. 26th Street
New York, NY 10001
(212) 366-9176
Website: https://chelsea.ucbtheatre.com
Like the UBC theaters in the East Village (https://east.ucbtheatre.com) and California (https://sunset.ucbtheatre.com and https://franklin.ucbtheatre.com), the oldest UBC hub features improv shows almost every night of the week, usually at $5 to $10 per show and sometimes featuring famous improv guests, including current *SNL* stars.

Websites

Because of the changing nature of Internet links, Rosen Publishing has developed an online list of websites related to the subject of this book. This site is updated regularly. Please use this link to access this list:

http://www.rosenlinks.com/COMEDY/Poeh

For Further Reading

Becker, Ron, Nick Marx, and Matt Sienkiewicz, eds. *Saturday Night Live and American TV*. Bloomington, IN: Indiana University Press, 2013.

Burnett, Carol. *This Time Together: Laughter and Reflection*. New York, NY: Three Rivers Press, 2011.

Castle, Alison, ed. Saturday Night Live: *The Book*. New York, NY: Taschen, 2015.

Dratch, Rachel. *Girl Walks into a Bar: Comedy Calamities, Dating Disasters, and a Midlife Miracle.* New York, NY: Gotham, 2013.

Fey, Tina. *Bossypants*. New York, NY: Sphere/Little, Brown and Co., 2011.

Halpern, Charna, and Del Close. *Truth in Comedy: The Manual for Improvisation.* Colorado Springs, CO: Meriwether Publishing, 1994.

Knope, Leslie. *Pawnee: The Greatest Town in America.* New York, NY: Hyperion, 2011.

Larson, Sarah. "Amy Poehler's Confidence Lessons." *New Yorker*, November 18, 2014. Retrieved May 23, 2015 (http://www.newyorker.com/culture/sarah-larson/amy-poehlers-confidence-lessons).

Martin, Steve. *Born Standing Up: A Comic's Life*. New York, NY: Scribner, 2008.

Miller, James Andrew, and Tom Shales. *Live From New York: The Complete, Uncensored History of* Saturday Night Live *as Told by Its Stars*,

Writers, and Guests. New York, NY: Little, Brown and Co., 2014.

Radner, Gilda. *It's Always Something.* 20th Anniversary Edition. New York, NY: Simon & Schuster, 2009.

Sedaris, Amy. *Simple Times: Crafts for Poor People*. New York, NY: Grand Central Publishing, 2010.

Short, Martin. *I Must Say: My Life as a Humble Comedy Legend.* New York, NY: Harper, 2015.

Thomas, Mike. *The Second City Unscripted: Revolution and Revelation at the World Famous Comedy Theater*. Evanston, IL: Northwestern University Press, 2012.

Walsh, Matt, Ian Roberts, and Matt Besser. *Upright Citizens Brigade Comedy Improvisational Manual*. New York, NY: Comedy Council of Nicea, 2013.

Bibliography

Anderson, Hephzibah. "Amy Poehler: Sweet Queen of Comedy with a Wicked Streak." *Observer*, October 18, 2014. Retrieved May 25, 2015 (http://www.theguardian.com/theobserver/2014/oct/19/amy-poehler-sweet-queen-comedy-wicked-streak).

Biography Online. "Carol Burnett, Biography." Retrieved May 25, 2015 (http://www.biography.com/people/carol-burnett-9231937#synopsis).

Blistein, Jon. "Golden Globes 2015: Tina Fey and Amy Poehler Roast Hollywood One Last Time." *Rolling Stone*, January 11, 2015. Retrieved May 23, 2015 (http://www.rollingstone.com/tv/features/golden-globes-2015-tina-fey-amy-poehler-monologue-20150111).

Bolonik, Kera. "Welcome to Her Island." *New York*, May 15, 2011. Retrieved May 23, 2015 (http://nymag.com/arts/tv/upfronts/2011/amy-poehler-2011-5).

Businesswire. "Amy Poehler and Friends Launch New Digital TV Show Aimed at Smart Girls and Their Parents." Retrieved May 23, 2015 (http://www.businesswire.com/news/home/20080918005279/en/Amy-Poehler-Friends-Launch-Digital-TV-Show#.VWN0SUb-QO9V).

Cardarelli, Lindsey. "Burlington's Amy Poehler Brings Local Laughs." *Woburn Daily Times Chronicle*, November 5, 2000. Retrieved May

25, 2015 (http://www.woburnonline.com/front-page/november05/11105-4.html).

Clark, Cindy. "Amy Poehler and Will Arnett Have Split." *USA Today*, September 6, 2012. Retrieved May 25, 2015 (http://content.usatoday.com/communities/entertainment/post/2012/09/amy-poehler-and-will-arnett-have-split/1#.VWN5f0bQO9V).

Combe, Rachel. "Amy Poehler Talks Feminism, Friendship, and Staying Away from Selfies." *Elle*, January 30, 2014. Retrieved May 23, 2015 (http://www.elle.com/culture/celebrities/a6/amy-poehler-women-in-tv-2014-interview).

Couric, Katie. "Amy Poehler Tells Katie Couric, 'I Just Love Bossy Women." *Glamour*, March 29, 2011. Retrieved May 23, 2015 (http://www.glamour.com/sex-love-life/2011/04/amy-poehler-tells-katie-couric-i-just-love-bossy-women).

Cruz, Gilbert. "Watch Tina Fey and Amy Poehler's Hilarious Golden Globes Monologue." *Vulture*, November 2014. Retrieved May 23, 2015 (http://www.vulture.com/2014/01/watch-tina-fey-amy-poehler-golden-globes-monologue.html).

Fey, Tina. *Bossypants*. New York, NY: Sphere/Little, Brown and Co., 2011.

Fox, Jesse David. "The History of Tina Fey and Amy Poehler's Best Friendship." *Vulture*, January

8, 2015. Retrieved May 24, 2015 (http://www.
vulture.com/2013/01/history-of-tina-and-amys-
best-friendship.html).

Gardner, Dwight. "S.N.L. Memories and Getting-
Some-Rest Dreams." *New York Times*, November 4, 2014. Retrieved May 25, 2015 (http://
www.nytimes.com/2014/11/05/books/book-
review-amy-poehlers-yes-please.html?_r=0).

Graser, Mark. "Legendary Entertainment Buys Amy
Poehler's Smart Girls at the Party." *Variety,* October 13, 2014. Retrieved May 23, 2015 (http://
variety.com/2014/digital/news/legendary-enter-
tainment-buys-amy-poehler-smart-girls-at-the-
party-1201328807).

Huffington Post. "Amy Poehler Gives Birth, No More
SNL." November 25, 2008. Retrieved May 23,
2015 (http://www.huffingtonpost.com/2008/10/
25/amy-poehler-gives-birth-n_n_137867.html).

Inside the Actor's Studio, featuring Amy Poehler,
2009 (TV).

Internet Movie Database. "Amy Poehler." Retrieved
May 25, 2015 (http://www.imdb.com/name/
nm0688132).

Internet Movie Database. "Conan O'Brien." Retrieved May 25, 2015 (http://www.imdb.com/
name/nm0005277/?ref_=nv_sr_1).

Internet Movie Database. "Del Close." Retrieved
May 23, 2015 (http://www.imdb.com/name/
nm0167081/?ref_=fn_al_nm_1).

Internet Movie Database. "Gilda Radner." Retrieved May 25, 2015 (http://www.imdb.com/name/nm0705717/).

Internet Movie Database. "Jane Curtain." Retrieved May 25, 2015 (http://www.imdb.com/name/nm0004852/?ref_=nv_sr_1).

Internet Movie Database. "Lorne Michaels." Retrieved May 23, 2015 (http://www.imdb.com/name/nm0167081/?ref_=fn_al_nm_1).

Larson, Sarah. "Amy Poehler's Confidence Lessons." *New Yorker,* November 18, 2014. Retrieved May 25, 2015 (http://www.newyorker.com/culture/sarah-larson/amy-poehlers-confidence-lessons).

Laudadio, Marisa. "Amy Poehler Gives Birth to Baby Boy." *People*, October 26, 2008. Retrieved May 25, 2015 (http://www.people.com/people/article/0,,20235875,00.html).

Los Angeles Times. "Golden Globes 2013: Tina Fey and Amy Poehler Raise to the Bar." January 14, 2013. Retrieved May 24, 2015 (http://articles.latimes.com/2013/jan/14/entertainment/la-et-st-golden-globes-review-fey-poehler-20130114).

McGlynn, Katia. "Tina Fey, Amy Poehler and Jane Curtain Return to 'Weekend Update Desk' for 'SNL' 40 Show." *Huffington Post*, February 15, 2015. Retrieved May 24, 2015 (http://www.huffingtonpost.com/2015/02/15/tina-fey-amy-poehler-jane-curtin-weekend-update-snl-40_n_6689714.html).

McNamara, Mary. "Cast of 'Parks and Rec' Off to Greener Pastures." *Los Angeles Time*s, February 24, 2015. Retrieved May 23, 2015 (http://www.latimes.com/entertainment/tv/la-et-st-parks-and-rec-finale-review-20150224-column.html).

Miller, Laura. "*Yes, Please* by Amy Poehler Review: Beefs, Advice, and Memoir." *Guardian*, November 26, 2014. Retrieved May 25, 2015 (http://www.theguardian.com/books/2014/nov/26/yes-please-amy-poehler-review-memoir).

NPR. "A Candid Memoir from Comedian Amy Poehler? *Yes, Please*." *Fresh Air*, October 28, 2014. Retrieved May 23, 2015 (http://www.npr.org/2014/10/28/359566469/a-candid-memoir-from-comedian-amy-poehler-yes-please).

NPR. "Amy Poehler's World of Local Government." *Fresh Air*, May 7, 2009. Retrieved May 25, 2015 (http://www.npr.org/templates/story/story.php?storyId=103879842).

Oldenburg, Ann. "Conan Makes TV History in Cuba." *USA Today,* February 16, 2015. Retrieved May 25, 2015 (http://www.usatoday.com/story/life/tv/2015/02/16/conan-films-in-cuba-first-late-night-host/23485345).

Poehler, Amy. *Yes, Please*. New York, NY: HarperCollins Publishers, 2014.

Scordelis, Alex. "Chasing Amy." *Paper*, December 2013. Retrieved May 24, 2015 (http://www.papermag.com/2013/12/amy_poehler_is_one_busy_lady.php).

Sherrill, Stephen. "Meet the Parents: The Poehlers." *Wall Street Journal*, February 25, 2011. Retrieved May 23, 2015 (http://www.wsj.com/articles/SB10001424052748704364004576132253325438900).

Storey, Kate. "The Poehler Siblings Are Ruling the Comedy World." *New York Post*, June 29, 2014. Retrieved May 24, 2015 (http://nypost.com/2014/06/29/the-poehler-siblings-are-ruling-the-comedy-world).

Theboot.com. "Tina Fey and Amy Poehler Respond to Taylor Swift's 'Special Place in Hell' Comment." March 6, 2013. Retrieved May 25, 2015 (http://theboot.com/tina-fey-amy-poehler-taylor-swift).

Worldwide Orphans Foundation. "Dr. Jane Aronson—bio." Retrieved May 24, 2015 (http://www.wwo.org/document.doc?id=281).

Wright, Megan. "Saturday Night's Children: Amy Poehler (2001–2008)." Splitsider Online, February 8, 2012. Retrieved May 23, 2015 (http://splitsider.com/2012/02/saturday-nights-children-amy-poehler-2001-2008).

Index

A

Aronson, Jane, 79, 80–81
Arnett, Will, 64, 70
Arrested Development, 64

B

Baby Mama, 70
Belushi, John, 24, 31, 69
Besser, Matt, 35, 38, 39, 48
Blades of Glory, 64
Bossypants, 56, 65
Boston College, 7, 18, 22, 26
Broad City, 82
Burnett, Carol, 7, 15–16

C

Carell, Steve, 27, 29
Clinton, Hillary, 8, 57, 60, 62, 64, 65
Close, Del, 31, 32, 41
Colbert, Stephen, 27, 29, 31
Comedy Central, 27, 29, 47, 49, 82
Compass Players, the, 21, 31
Curtain, Jane, 68–69

D

Deuce Bigalow: Male Gigolo, 45
Dratch, Rachel, 52

E

Emmy Awards, 16, 24, 29, 43, 69, 75, 76

F

Ferrell, Will, 52, 64
Fey, Tina, 31, 33, 50–51, 54, 56, 57, 59, 60, 64, 65, 68, 70, 75, 76, 77, 82

G

Golden Globes, 75, 77

H

Halpern, Charna, 32, 33

I

improvisational theater (improv), 7–8, 13, 20, 21, 23, 25, 26–27, 29–30, 31, 32–33, 35, 37, 40–41, 43, 54, 56, 57, 59, 60
ImprovOlympic (iO), 7, 25, 29, 30, 32–33, 35
the Family, 32, 35

K

Kroll, Nick, 82

L

Late Night with Conan O'Brien, 42, 43

M

McCarthy, Melissa, 69, 76
McNamara, Kara, 20, 22, 23, 25, 26
Mean Girls, 70
Meyers, Seth, 32–33, 54, 60, 64–65, 66
Michaels, Lorne, 50, 52, 53–54, 55–56, 64
Milmore, Steve and Helen, 10
Murray, Bill, 24, 31, 69
My Mother's Fleabag, 20

O

O'Brien, Conan, 29, 42, 43–44
Once Upon a Mattress, 16

P

Palin, Sarah, 57, 60, 62, 64–65
Parks and Recreation, 71, 75
Parnell, Chris, 54
Poehler, Amy
  birth of children, 66, 68
  charitable work, 78–81
  childhood, 9–14
  college, 18–25
  comedy career in Chicago, 26–37

high school, 14, 16–17
impersonation of Hillary Clinton, 57–64
as inspiration to young women, 8, 9, 77–79
as member of SNL, 51–67
as member of UCB, 35–49
post-SNL career, 71–77, 82–83
Poehler, Bill, 9–10, 12, 13, 18, 25, 26, 47, 52, 73
Poehler, Eileen, 9–10, 12, 13, 18, 25, 47, 52, 57, 73
Poehler, Greg, 12, 13, 42, 82

R

Radner, Gilda, 7, 23–24, 31, 69
Richter, Andy, 45
Roberts, Ian, 35, 48
Rudolph, Maya, 52, 66, 82

S

Sanz, Horatio, 52
Saturday Night Live (SNL), 7, 8, 23–24, 31, 32, 43, 45, 50–70, 73, 76, 82
  production schedule, 52, 54–56

sketches impersonating Hillary Clinton and Sarah Palin, 57, 59, 60–65
Second City, 7, 21, 23, 27, 31, 33, 37, 50
Sedaris, Amy, 27, 29, 31
Sedaris, David, 27, 28
September 11, 49, 51
Shannon, Molly, 52
Sisters, 82
Smart Girls, 8, 78–79
South Park, 47
Swift, Taylor, 77

T
30 Rock, 54, 64
Tomorrow Night, 45

U
Upright Citizens Brigade (UCB), 7, 35–42, 45, 51, 57, 81
Comedy Central show, 47–49

W
Walsh, Matt, 35, 48
"Weekend Update," 50, 59, 60, 65, 66, 68, 69
Welcome to Sweden, 82
Wet Hot American Summer, 45, 82

Wiig, Kristen, 52, 76
women representation in media, 62, 77
Worldwide Orphans Foundation, 79, 80, 81

Y
Yes, Please, 10, 12, 20, 22, 30, 33, 35, 51, 78

About the Author

Justine Ciovacco has written more than sixty nonfiction books and hundreds of articles on biography, science, history, and current events topics for young people. Her writing has been published by Discovery Channel School Books, Scholastic, Reader's Digest Books for Young Families, National Geographic, Time for Kids, Dorling Kindersley, SmartLab, and Disney, among others. She has been a volunteer with children at the New York City branch of Gilda's Club, the cancer wellness community inspired by *SNL* legend Gilda Radner, since 1998, and serves as a preliminary judge for the "It's Always Something" Essay Contest for teens.

Photo Credits

Cover, p. 3 s_bukley/Shutterstock.com; cover background, interior pages (curtain) Kostsov/Shutterstock.com; p. 6 Alberto E. Rodriguez/Getty Images; p. 11 George Pimentel/WireImage/Getty Images; p. 15 John Heller/WireImage/Getty Images; p. 17 Ron Case/Hulton Archive/Getty Images; p. 19 The Boston Globe/ Getty Images; pp. 24, 69 Ron Galella/Ron Galella Collection/Getty Images; p. 28 Desiree Navarro/WireImage/Getty Images; pp. 34, 53 Jason LaVeris/FilmMagic/ Getty Images; p. 36 Vincent Sandoval/WireImage/Getty Images; p. 39 Daniel Zuchnik/FilmMagic/Getty Images; p. 44 Lester Cohen/WireImage/Getty Images; pp. 46-47 Hulton Archive/Getty Images; p. 55 Sylvain Gaboury/FilmMagic/ Getty Images; p. 58 Getty Images; p. 61 Larry Busacca/Getty Images; pp. 62-63 Timothy A. Clary/AFP/Getty Images; p. 67 Jean Baptiste Lacroix/WireImage/ Getty Images; pp. 72-73 Frederick M. Brown/Getty Images; p. 74 Jason Merritt/ Getty Images; p. 80 Jason Kempin/Getty Images.

Designer: Nicole Russo; Editor: Tracey Baptiste; Photo Research: Bruce Donnola